The his LOTUS in FORMULA 1

to the rhythm of fast lap

Charles Sanz

INTRODUCTION

Lotus is one of the most legendary manufacturers in Formula 1, and one of those that has revolutionized the competition the most throughout its history with innovations such as the use of ground effect or the incorporation of active suspension, as a result of the genius from its founder: Colin Chapman.

The history of Lotus is that of a team with constant innovations that was born and grew at the end of the 50s through drivers like Cliff Allison or Innes Ireland to achieve glory through a legend like Jim Clark, being the first constructor in build a one-piece chassis.

Lotus came to dominate Formula 1 in the 70s, with its magnificent single-seaters being driven by great drivers such as Graham Hill, Jochen Rindt or Emerson Fittipaldi. Taking advantage of the ground effect of the Lotus 78, the competition surrendered to the ingenuity of a team that led Andretti to become champion.

After its best stage, Lotus continued to fight to win championships again, counting on future legends such as Nigel Mansell or Ayrton Senna. However, the legendary team had to face a progressive decline, and a difficult return in search of past glory.

In this book you will discover in an entertaining way the main keys to the history of this magnificent constructor, to remember or enjoy one of the most successful and legendary teams in the greatest motor racing competition.

I hope you enjoy the following pages, and enjoy the story of a team that, although part of Formula 1's past, has sown passion in many of its fans who continue to eagerly await a new comeback.

Colin Chapman and the origin of the Lotus

If there is a name associated with Lotus in Formula 1, that is Colin Chapman, the founder of the brand and the team.

Anthony Colin Bruce Champan was born on May 19, 1928 in Richmond, England. The son of the manager of The Railway hotel in Tottenham Lane, he spent his childhood at a Mayfield Road school, after which he was admitted to the University of London Air Squadron, where he studied structural engineering.

In 1948 he was enlisted in the Royal Air Force, but after refusing a lifetime commission, he gave up his military career.

He worked mainly for the British Aluminum company, where he applied his knowledge as an engineer in his work as a salesman to introduce aluminum in the construction of houses.

1

However, life had a space saved for him in motorsport. In 1948, he designed the Mk1, a variant of the Austin 7, with which he began to participate in local races. He named his car Lotus. It is believed that he used this name since he used to call his girlfriend Hazel as "lotus flower".

As he gained competitions and his financial resources increased, he developed the Lotus Mk2. It was an evolution of the Mk1 (and therefore the Austin 7) with an improved chassis and crossmembers using stronger tubular stays.

---

[1]motorsportmagazine.com

He also replaced the engine, beginning to use first the Ford 8 and later the Ford 10. From his early years as a car designer, Chapman was noted for his ability to stay on the edge of regulation in order to improve his vehicles.

In 1952 he decided to found his own car company: Lotus Engineering Ltd. (later to be renamed Lotus Cars). It was a personal project to which he dedicated his free time along with other fans. The company stood out for creating cars based on good handling over power. Chapman claimed that the power provided more speed on the straights, but a more manageable car allowed for better speed on all sides.

However, Chapman did not put aside his competitive passion and created the competition-oriented Team Lotus team in 1954, to differentiate it from the Lotus Cars company dedicated to the commercial creation of automobiles.

With the continuous development of its racing car one version after

_____

[2]Motorhistory.com

another, even its competitive versions ended up being sold, so that the chassis of the Lotus Mark VI was sold so that its buyers could install their favorite engine and gearbox, reaching exceed one hundred units sold. The Lotus 7 increased sales of its competition designs even further.

Chapman even competed in Formula 1, participating with Vanwall in the 1956 French Grand Prix. However, during practice he collided with his teammate Mike Hawthorn, which led him to give up as a driver to focus on his career as an engineer. and creator of single-seaters.

In this way, in 1958 Champan decided to register its own team to participate in Formula 1. Thus began Lotus's career in the largest motorsport competition.

After the first years of the competition, dominated by Alfa Romeo, Ferrari, Mercedes and Maserati, Chapman would go on to become one of the most important representatives of the rise of British brands in Formula 1.

[3]

[3]statsf1.com

Lotus debut in Formula 1

In 1958, the ninth edition of the Formula 1 world championship, Team Lotus debuted in competition with the Lotus 12. The single-seater complied with Chapman's philosophy of creating a manageable car, focusing on reducing its weight and on aerodynamic improvement.

He sought to place the pilot as low as possible, reducing the height of the gearbox and moving it to the rear. This gearbox suffered from oil problems which were slow to be resolved, compromising the reliability of the Lotus 12.

The Lotus 12 wheels were innovative by using a magnesium alloy, which sought to further lighten the car, giving rise to the striking oscillating band wheels.

The car had a Coventry Climax FPF 2.0 L4 engine, which would later be replaced by the FPF 2.2 L4 incorporated into the Lotus 16 that would be used from the sixth race of the year.

The new Lotus 16 bore many similarities to the Vanwall, which Chapman had learned during his time with the British team. This led to him earning the nickname of mini Vanwall. The design improved upon the Lotus 12's fundamentals, with its gearbox traveling to the side of the driver rather than underneath to give the driver more room, allowing him to sit in a distinctive reclining stance. A bulge was also added behind the cockpit to reposition and increase the capacity of the fuel tank.

4

The drivers chosen to drive these first two Lotus versions in their first season in Formula 1 were Cliff Allison and Graham Hill. The two Britons had no experience in the newly created Formula 1, so they made their debut in the category with the Lotus team.

However, the two pilots already had a previous relationship with Chapman, who had discovered them in the lower categories and had made them Lotus pilots in other competitions (in fact, Allison shared with Chapman himself the Lotus with which they ended up in sixth position at the 12 Hours of Sebring in 1958 before debuting in Formula 1).

Lotus' debut in Formula 1 finally took place on May 18, 1958 in Monaco, the second date of the season. Graham Hill was unable to finish the race after a broken axle. However, Cliff Allison was able to finish in sixth position, although 13 laps behind the leader, he being the last driver able to finish the demanding race.

This meant a moderate debut for Lotus, but an encouraging one, as

[5]soymotor.com

Collins was only one position away from having scored the first points for the team.

In the second race in the Netherlands, the result would be identical. Allison was sixth, and Graham Hill retired again, this time with temperature issues. In fact, Hill would end up abandoning one race after another, chaining seven consecutive abandonments, being able to finish only the last two races: Italy and Morocco. In the Italian event he was sixth and in Morocco he was 16th, so he finished the season with no points.

6

As for Allison, in his third race he finished fourth, behind only the three drivers who took the podium: Tony Brooks, Mike Hawthorn and Stuart Lewis-Evans. With this fourth position, Allison achieved the first three points of Team Lotus in Formula 1.

In fact, they would be the last points for Lotus in the entire season. The introduction of the Lotus 16 failed to improve performance.

In the remaining six races, Allison retired in half of them, finishing in the top ten in the remaining three, but failing to return to points.

On the sixth round of the British race, driver Alan Stacey replaced Allison, but would eventually drop out.

In this way, Lotus finished in the sixth position of constructors in its first year in the competition, being the last brand in the classification that had participated almost completely in the calendar, behind Vanwall, Ferrari, Cooper, BRM and Maserati. .

In the table, it only surpassed Porsche, Connaught and OSCA, brands that had appeared only occasionally in the competition.

In 1959, Team Lotus participated the entire season with the Lotus 16 Climax FPF 2.5 L4.

Other private drivers or teams would also end up using the Lotus 12 or Lotus 16 chassis privately such as Bruce Halford, Dennis Taylor or David Piper.

As for the official team, Chapman lost Cliff Allison, the driver who had scored the first points for the team, since he went on to drive for Ferrari.

Graham Hill's main teammate on this occasion in Team Lotus was Englishman Innes Ireland. After two years participating in national competitions, Chapman gave him the opportunity to debut in Formula 1.

In addition to its two main drivers, Team Lotus had the American Pete Lovely for the first race in Monaco and the British Alan Stacey who this time extended his participation with the team to two events: Great Britain and the United States.

The driver who obtained the best performance from the Lotus 16 was Innes Ireland, who with a fourth position in the Netherlands and a fifth position in the United States, achieved a total of 5 points for the team. The remaining four races he entered, he had to retire showing the unreliability of the Lotus.

[7]sportscars.tv
[8]pinterest.co.uk

Ireland's points were the only points Lotus could get. As for Graham Hill, after retiring in five of the seven races he entered, he could only finish seventh in the Netherlands and ninth in Great Britain.

Pete Lovely failed to qualify for his only Monaco race and Stacey was eighth in Great Britain, retiring in the USA.

Of the rest of the private drivers who chose to use the Lotus this season, none managed to finish any race.

With Ireland's 5 points, Lotus secured fourth position in the final manufacturers' standings. This time it was not the last team of the regulars in the competition, surpassing Cooper-Maserati, showing a slight improvement, although still far from the brands that dominated the competition: Cooper-Climax, Ferrari and BRM.

The brilliant decade of the 60s and the legend of Jim Clark

For the 1960 season, Team Lotus developed the Lotus 18 model with the aim of continuing to progress in the competition. The main characteristic of the new single-seater was that it incorporated an engine in a central position.

This innovation had already been successfully incorporated by Cooper, taking the first win in a mid-engined Formula 1 car two years earlier via the Cooper T43. Since then, designers have debated whether to continue using the front engine or to adopt the new mid-engine dynamics. Ferrari was one of the teams that took the longest to adopt the mid-engine, which caused it to fall behind for a while.

Again, Chapman opted for maneuverability over his Climax FPF 2.5

L4 engine, achieving good handling through a tubular chassis made up of lightweight bolt-on panels that gave it an almost triangular appearance where the rider's position continued to force him to be slightly lying down.

For this new season, Lotus managed to keep Innes Ireland, its best driver from the previous season, and extended Alan Stacey's participation to four races.

Apart from them, the team opted for a large squad to exchange their drivers throughout the year. One of those most prominent pilots was John Surtees.

Having won three motorcycle world championships, the Englishman wanted to compete in Formula 1 to further his legend, and Chapman gave him the opportunity to try to shine in a different discipline than he was used to.

_____

[9]Pinterest.com.mx

10

In the middle part of the championship, Surtees had to be absent to focus on the motorcycle world championship (which he would also win that year), and was replaced by Scotsman Jim Clark. Until then, Clark had participated in the rally category and in local races.

11

[10]Motorhistory.com
[11]thesporting.blog

In addition, the team had occasional collaborations such as that of the Argentine Alberto Rodríguez Larreta in his homeland or that of Ron Flockhart in the Belgian test.

In addition to the factory team, the Lotus 18 was also driven by privateer drivers such as Mike Taylor and Jim Hall.

The season started with a decent sixth place for Innes Ireland in Argentina. In the second round in Monaco, he was ninth, with John Surtees having to retire (and would not return until the final part of the championship).

After the stoppage of the Indianapolis 500 (where practically no Formula 1 team participated despite being eligible for the championship), the competition traveled to the Netherlands, already with Jim Clark as part of the squad.

At the Zandvoort circuit, Innes Ireland achieved their best result and also that of Lotus, achieving a magnificent second position that was the first podium finish for the team. Ireland trailed 24 seconds behind Jack Brabham's Cooper who led every lap of the race.

12

Ireland's podium finish was not a one-time success, as he took two

12alodecals.wordpress.com

more podium finishes, finishing third in Great Britain and second again in the United States, adding a total of 18 points that allowed him to finish fourth in the final drivers' standings.

Meanwhile, Jim Clark also managed to get to the podium in Portugal, as well as finishing fifth in the races in Belgium and France, which brought more points to the team.

On his return late in the championship, John Surtees also gave the Lotus team one more podium finish, finishing second in Great Britain.

This new dynamic for Team Lotus, which became a team frequently on the podium, allowed the manufacturer to finish second in the final standings, 14 points behind the indomitable Cooper. This runner-up position (above Ferrari), encouraged the team to take the next step: win the first race and, why not, aspire to the world title.

For the year 1961 and with the aim of trying to achieve the first victory, the Lotus 18 was incorporating innovations until it became the Lotus 21, whose main characteristic was the evolution of its spatial structure covered with fiberglass.

[13]

[13]carpixel.net

Innes Ireland and Jim Clark were the team's two main drivers for the entire season in a shorter squad, also featuring Trevor Taylor for the Dutch test and Belgian Willy Mairesse in France.

Other teams also used the Lotus 21 such as the famed Walker Racing Team driven by Stirling Moss, with the legendary Briton taking the first victory for a Lotus, albeit in a different team than the factory one.

Many teams continued to rely on the Lotus 18 to participate this year, such as Scuderia Colonia, Equipe Nationale Belge, Camoradi International, Laystall Racing Team, Tony Marsh, Tim Parnell, Gerry Ashmore, Louise Bryden-Brown, Gaetano Starraba, J. Wheeler Autosport, Jim Hall or J. Frank Harrison. This demonstrated the confidence of the participants in the British constructor.

The season started with Stirling Moss winning in Monaco in the Walker Racing Team Lotus, while Ireland failed to even start the race and Jim Clark was tenth.

This season was a difficult one for Innes Ireland, having to retire in the middle of the races, with a fourth position in France the best result not being enough consolation.

Meanwhile, Jim Clark managed to keep Team Lotus on the podium by finishing third in the Netherlands and France.

When it already seemed that the season would end up being a slight step back for the team, with two podium finishes as satisfactory results, in the final test in the United States, Innes Ireland once again gave the Lotus team joy by crossing the finish line first after a tough battle with Dan Gurney's Porsche.

Ireland's win at Watkins Glen gave the Lotus factory team their first win, as they were finally celebrating their first grand prix win.

14

Together with the two victories for Stirling Moss for Lotus, the British constructor returned to achieve a new runner-up, 8 points behind Ferrari, which did not even need to participate in the last race.

The runner-up was repeated, but the first victory in a race was achieved and the illusion of winning a world championship in the future continued.

With the aim of continuing to aspire to more triumphs, Team Lotus developed the Lotus 24 for the year 1962. This model was quickly replaced by the Lotus 25. Despite the successes of the model 24 in the races prior to the championship, they felt that soon could become obsolete and was improved to model 25.

The Lotus 25 was a revolution since it was the first single-seater with

[14]second-a-lap.blogspot.com

a monocoque chassis, manufactured in a single piece. The resistance of this new monocoque tripled that of the Lotus 24, and its height, being lower than the rest of the vehicles on the grid, gave it exceptional maneuverability and aerodynamics.

15

Innes Ireland left the Lotus factory team to which he had brought so many achievements to join the UDT Laystall Racing Team, which would end up using the Lotus 24.

Jim Clark remained in the official team, and his only companion was the British Trevor Taylor. Taylor had participated in just two Formula 1 races, failing to qualify for Great Britain in 1959 and finishing 13th in the Netherlands in 1961.

---

[15]ar.pinterest.com

Again, numerous teams returned to use the Lotus, including the prestigious Walker Racing Team. However, most of them had bought units of the Lotus 24, so they were surprised when the factory team ended up developing the new Lotus 25, thinking that they would participate with the same car.

Thus the season started satisfactorily with a second position for Trevor Taylor in the Netherlands, only behind an old Lotus acquaintance: Graham Hill, who was now driving a BRM for the Owen Racing Organization team.

Monaco was a difficult race for Team Lotus, with Clark and Taylor retiring, but on round three in Belgium, the 'flying Scotsman' took his first victory in Belgium, leading Lotus to glory once again.

It was not the only victory for Jim Clark that year, who repeated triumphs in Great Britain and the United States, which led him to win the drivers' second championship behind a Graham Hill who, with four victories and two second places, was unattainable.

---

[16]formula1points.com

Despite Trevor Taylor's good start, the rest of the season his performance slowed down, failing to finish above eighth position.

This prevented Lotus from fighting for the constructors' championship, although they returned to add a new runner-up just six points behind BRM. The constructor returned to repeat the second final position in the championship, but the sensations were good having achieved three victories, with a Jim Clark who seemed to improve by leaps and bounds.

For the 1963 season, Team Lotus continued to rely on the Lotus 25 and its long relationship with Climax engines, this time with the FWMV 1.5 V8 model.

This time, this model was used by another team on the grid, the Brabham Racing Organisation, with the rest of the private teams keeping the Lotus 24 (the Walker Racing Team had chosen to use Cooper single-seaters).

Jim Clark and Trevor Taylor continued to be the two main drivers of the team, with the collaboration of the Mexican Pedro Rodríguez in two races and the occasional appearances of the British Peter Arundell and Mike Spence.

The season began with Taylor finishing sixth in Monaco and Jim Clark eighth in what was a slightly worrying start. However, the doubts dissipated from the second date.

Jim Clark was victorious in the next four races: Belgium, Holland, France and Great Britain. In Germany he was overtaken by John Surtees' Ferrari, but immediately returned to victory in Italy. After a third place finish in the United States, he finished the season with two more victories: Mexico and South Africa.

With the exception of his eighth place in Monaco, Jim Clark managed to climb to the podium in all the remaining races, adding a total of seven victories that made him world champion with a great advantage over Graham Hill. The Scotsman's superiority was indisputable, doubling the majority of the grid in many of the races.

Jim Clark's success was transferred to Lotus as a constructor, which managed to dominate the classification table and achieve the first world constructors' title, well above brands such as BRM, Brabham, Ferrari or Cooper. In a magnificent season, Lotus finally achieved absolute glory. From that moment on, the challenge of maintaining it began.

In 1964, Lotus began with the successful Lotus 25, although it would be replaced throughout the year by the Lotus 33 designed by Colin

[17]pinterest.es

Chapman and Len Terry. With a monocoque very similar to its predecessor, the new model sought to improve the suspension to accommodate larger tires.

18

With Trevor Taylor leaving the team to join the British Racing Partnership, Jim Clark's teammate at the start of the season was Peter Arundell.

The Briton had already tried to participate with Team Lotus in the previous two years in the French test, failing to start the race on both occasions.

---

[18]ultimatecarpage.com

Arundell made his debut on the podium taking third place in Monaco, with Jim Clark being fourth. Peter was once again on the podium in Holland, where this time the Scotsman was reunited with victory.

The first part of the championship looked like it would be a repeat of the previous season, with Jim Clark winning three of the first five races. However, Great Britain was a turning point for the team. After the British race, Jim Clark chained three consecutive retirements, and the two races that he managed to finish he could not improve the fifth position.

Meanwhile, Arundell picked up an injury in Great Britain and was replaced for the rest of the season by Mike Spence, who, although he managed a fourth in Mexico and sixth in Italy, failed to make the podium. This spelled a disastrous second half of the season for Team Lotus, with Jim Clark settling for third in the drivers' standings behind John Surtees and Graham Hill, and Lotus also finishing third in the manufacturers' position behind Ferrari and BRM.

The Lotus 33, in combination with the Lotus 25, returned to being the single-seaters used by Team Lotus in 1965, hoping to solve the

[19]motorsportmagazine.com

reliability problems that had prevented them from competing for the title the previous year.

Jim Clark continued to be the team's star driver, this time alongside Mike Spence, who, after participating in the second half of the previous season, had secured a spot with a full program this time around.

The reliability problems were solved and this allowed Jim Clark to unleash his full potential, winning the first six consecutive races (not counting the one in Monaco where Team Lotus did not appear), and putting on track a championship that no longer eluded him despite from his tenth place in Italy and his two DNFs in the final two races in the United States and Mexico.

With an undisputed start to the season, Jim Clark had built up enough of an advantage to clinch his second world championship in comfort.

[20]

Mike Spence only got a single podium, in the last race in the United States. He had previously been fourth in Great Britain and South Africa. Finally, he added 10 points to finish tenth in the final standings.

---

[20]roadandtrack.com

21

Despite Spence's scant contribution, Jim Clark's good results were enough for Lotus to win its second constructors' championship, faced with the threat of BRM, which threatened to snatch the victory from him, taking advantage of Lotus' bad final trend, achieving victory in Italy and the United States through Jackie Stewart and Graham Hill.

However, BRM was unable to complete the comeback and Lotus ended up clinching the constructors' world championship for the second time.

In 1966, Lotus continued to rely on the successful Lotus 33, although it would end up becoming the Lotus 43 in response to the new Formula 1 regulations, which established a new 3-liter capacity for engines and the use of wider wheels. .

Larger engine capacity required a beefier chassis, and Colin Chapman used his IndyCar knowledge to design it. In this model, the Climax

pinterest.es

engine was no longer used, with the intention of incorporating the DFV, but since it was not fully developed, it was decided to use a BRM P75 3.0 H16 engine. The DFV Cosworth engine was tested in the German race alongside an early draft of the Lotus 44.

22

For its part, the Reg Parnell Racing team used the Lotus 33 for Mike Spence, while Phil Hill used the Lotus 25 for his privateer team in the first race of the season.

Jim Clark was the star driver for Lotus for another year, alongside Peter Arundell, who had already driven the team for four races two years earlier.

The Mexican Pedro Rodríguez also had an expanded program with Lotus participating in four events. In 1963 he had already participated in two events with the team, before spending two seasons with the North American Racing Team where he scored his first points in the competition.

---

[22]roadandtrack.com

23

The German Gerhard Mitter and the British Piers Coruage also participated in Germany in the first appearance of the Lotus 44.

The season started with terrible mechanical problems. Jim Clark had to retire in the first two races, and in France he couldn't even start. Reliability problems were even more severe at Arundell, who failed to finish any of the first five races.

As reliability improved Jim Clark was able to put his talent to use, finishing fourth in Great Britain and a podium finish in the Netherlands, although DNFs continued to be frequent and the Scotsman was only able to claim victory in the USA. With these results, he added 16 points and the two-time champion was satisfied with the final fifth position in the championship.

[23]pinterest.es

His teammate Arundell could only get one point after finishing sixth in the United States, while Pedro Rodríguez ended up retiring in all four races he participated in.

This season, Lotus-BRM finished fifth in the constructors' standings in a dismal season in which the goal was to continue winning championships.

The disaster was mainly due to the weight of the BRM engine (it took four mechanics to get it off the truck when they received the first engine), which affected the handling of the rest of the design.

1967 was a year of uncertainty. Colin Chapman and Maurice Philippe developed the Lotus 49 around the DFV Cosworth engine. It was the first car to incorporate tension bars to lighten the weight of the engine (the main problem they had suffered the previous season), an innovation that would soon be replicated by the rest of the squad. The engine was anchored at one end and the suspension and gearbox at the other, a structure that was later adopted by all Formula 1 cars.

24

[24]pinterest.es

However, the development of the Ford Cosworth DFV 3.0 V8 engine continued to be delayed (an engine that Chapman himself had convinced Ford to build), so the season began with the Lotus 43, and the Lotus was even used again. 33.

Jim Clark was once again the benchmark in Team Lotus, and this season he was accompanied by Graham Hill, who was returning to the team in which he had made his competition debut after seven years driving the Owen Racing Organization BRM with which he had He was champion in 1962 and runner-up three times between 1963 and 1965. His fifth position in 1966, a year in which he failed to win, motivated him to return to Lotus.

Team Lotus thus had two drivers who already knew what it was like to win a championship.

25

In addition, the team had occasional participations from the Canadian Eppie Wietzes, the Italian Giancarlo Baghetti and the Mexican Moisés Solana.

This year the team was competitive, at least when reliability didn't ruin races again.

Clark had four wins throughout the year, plus one additional podium finish. They were again very good results, but up to five retirements prevented him from fighting for the championship, finally finishing third behind Denny Hulme and Jack Brabham.

In the case of Graham Hill, the reliability problems were even greater. He suffered eight retirements, being able to finish only three races, getting on the podium in two of them to finish seventh in the final standings.

As a constructor, Lotus rose to second position and achieved a new runner-up position, although far from the private Brabham team that managed to win the championship.

The good news was that most of the points had been achieved after the arrival of the Ford Cosworth engine and the Lotus 44. Lotus-Ford had achieved 44 points, compared to the 6 points achieved by the models that used the BRM engine or the old Climax. Reliability issues also diminished as the season progressed.

For these reasons, there was hope in aspiring to win new championships in the following seasons.

For the 1968 season, the Lotus 49 with the Ford Cosworth engine was already prepared for its first full season in Formula 1. It was even improved throughout the year, giving rise to the 49B version with innovations such as the addition of wings, being the first car to use the wings in competition.

The purpose of the wings was to achieve the opposite effect to airplanes, to "glue" the car to the ground, so that it could face the curves at higher speed.

These early wings were subject to suspensions, and were banned from racing until they were reinstated later, as long as they were attached to fixed parts of the car.

Champions Jim Clark and Graham Hill were repeat drivers, so with two talented drivers and a car that seemed to work, it was set to be a highly successful season for Team Lotus (renamed Gold Leaf Team Lotus for part of the campaign). , which for sponsorship reasons led him to abandon the classic green color and adopt red as the main color).

The first race in South Africa confirmed expectations, with Jim Clark taking victory and Graham Hill in second position, in a double that showed the superiority of the team.

However, soon after, the Lotus had a difficult season in the worst possible way. Between the first and second race of the year there was a 4-month difference, which the pilots took advantage of to participate in other categories.

Jim Clark meanwhile decided to participate in the Deutschland Trophäe for Lotus, a Formula 2 race at the Hockenheimring. On the

[26]statsf1.com

fifth lap, for unknown reasons (probably due to a flat rear tire), the legendary Scottish driver went off the track and collided with trees, which caused him to fracture his skull and neck, losing his life in the accident.

27

The loss of the legendary driver caused a great impact in the world of motorsports, and Colin Chapman himself assured that he had lost one of his best friends. Formula 1 lost one of the most outstanding drivers in its history.

From the third race, Jim Clark's place in Team Lotus was taken by the British Jackie Oliver. He thus debuted in Formula 1 after having

---

[27]scotsman.com

participated in Formula 2 the previous year with the Lotus Components Ltd. team, finishing fifth in the German test.

28

Despite the personal tragedy, Team Lotus managed to maintain sporting performance, with Graham Hill winning the next two races in Spain and Monaco. However, the rest of the season was not going to be so easy.

Despite twice podium finishes, Hill went eight races without victory. That allowed Jackie Stewart to close the gap with his Matra. For the last race in Mexico, Graham Hill's lead over Stewart was just three points.

In Mexico City, Graham Hill took third place on the starting grid, four positions ahead of Stewart. Despite this, Stewart managed to reach the top position on lap five, compromising Hill's championship... but the Matra's engine began to fail, leaving him with no chance of victory.

---

[28]f1forgottendrivers.com

Graham Hill then took the opportunity to achieve victory without any opposition and thus added his second world championship for drivers.

29

Jackie Oliver completed the season with a podium in Mexico as his best result, with many problems throughout the year not being able to start the events in the United States and France, not being able to qualify in the Netherlands and retiring in four races, with 6 final points that took him to position number 15 in the drivers' championship.

Despite this, Lotus obtained enough points to win the constructors'

[29]vavel.com

championship, with less suffering than the drivers'. With 13 points ahead of McLaren, Lotus achieved the third Formula 1 manufacturers' championship in its history.

To end the decade, Gold Leaf Team Lotus relied on the Lotus 49B for the 1969 season, continuing its association with the Ford Cosworth DFV that would eventually spread to almost the entire grid and become one of the most successful engines in the series. Formula 1 history.

Graham Hill continued in the team, accompanied mainly by the Austrian Jochen Rindt. Rindt had debuted in Formula 1 in the race of his country in 1964 with the Rob Walker Racing Team, having to leave. After that, he spent three years with Cooper where he took his first three podiums and finished third in the final drivers' standings in 1966. His move to Brabham in 1968 was not very successful, scoring two podiums but dropping out in all races. remaining races.

In 1969, he signed for Team Lotus with the aim of achieving his first victory in Formula 1.

30

[30]f1-fansite.com

Another driver who had extensive involvement with the team this season was John Miles. The Englishman had excelled in local races with a Diva-Austin GT, which led Colin Chapman to notice him and give him a chance in Formula 1.

American Mario Andretti also entered three races and Richard Altwood drove a Lotus for the Monaco event.

Graham Hill began the season with a second position in South Africa, and two races later he was victorious in Monaco. Meanwhile, Rindt was starting with four straight DNFs.

Graham Hill's season had a negative trend, and after his victory in Monaco he did not get on the podium again. Finally, the champion finished seventh in the final standings with 19 points, unable to compete with Jackie Stewart who this time dominated the competition with his Matra.

On the other hand, Jochen Rindt did improve his trend as soon as reliability allowed him, adding two podiums and a victory in the United States in the last four races of the year. This allowed him to add 22 points and move up to the final fourth position of drivers.

John Miles could only finish the race in Great Britain, in tenth position, retiring in his remaining four participations. Andretti also retired in all three of his starts in a mechanically disastrous season for Lotus.

These results relegated Lotus to the third final position in the Constructors' World Championship and meant another step back in his career. Like other times in which it had achieved glory, it was difficult for the British team to maintain success over time.

The golden 70s of Rindt, Fittipaldi and Andretti

In 1970, Gold Leaf Team Lotus (which would also end up using the Garvey Team Lotus and World Wide Racing names throughout the season), improved the Lotus 49 to obtain the 49C version (after failing to design the new Lotus 63).

These improvements would be insufficient to recover the maximum level, so the new Lotus 72 was quickly incorporated in the early stages of the season.

With the wings limited to easily detaching and causing incidents, Colin Chapman and Maurice Philippe began development of the Lotus 72 with the intention of taking advantage of the aerodynamic effect despite having to limit the height and size of the wings. To do this, they devised the innovative wedge shape of the chassis and the angled layout of the car. Along with an innovative repositioning of the radiators from the front to the sides, the seeds of a champion car had been sown.

The brake and ignition problems that the new car showed were resolved throughout the year until its 72B and 72C versions were found, which would also be used by the Rob Walker Racing Team.

31

With Graham Hill having signed for the Rob Walker team, Jochen Rindt remained as the main driver for the factory team, alongside John Miles, who this time would participate throughout the campaign looking to improve on his results from the previous year.

This year Lotus also made an addition that would end up being key in its future. The Brazilian Emerson Fittipaldi would debut in Formula 1 participating with Team Lotus in five races.

The British team would also have the participation of the Spanish

[31]motorpassion.com

Alex Soler-Roig in three events and the Swedish Reine Wisell in two.

The season did not start in the best way for Lotus, with a fifth place for Miles in South Africa and a 13th position for Rindt, and the second race in Spain did not bode well for the team either with the Austrian retiring and Miles failing to finish. time required to qualify.

However, in Monaco, Jochen Rindt's victory would dispel doubts, and despite retiring in Belgium, the Austrian achieved four consecutive victories in the Netherlands, France, Great Britain and Germany that returned Lotus to glory and maximized the prospects. expectations.

However, as quickly as the illusion had returned to the team, it fizzled out in the tenth round in Italy.

During practice at Monza, Rindt's car lost direction and went straight into the Parabolica corner, crashing into the wall.

Jochen broke his legs and parts of the car struck his chest and abdomen, killing him shortly afterwards.

32

---

[32]modestino.blogspot.com

After his death, Jochen Rindt led the championship with a 20-point advantage over his pursuers, with only four races to go including the Italian event.

Despite his absence, no driver was able to achieve the consistency necessary to close the gap and in the United States, the penultimate round of the year, Rindt still held a 14-point lead over the Belgian Jacky Ickx, second placed.

This meant that Jochen Rindt automatically became world champion, being the only driver to become champion posthumously.

33

As for his teammate, John Miles, he decided to leave the team after Rindt's death, becoming a BRM test driver and racing touring cars until his final retirement three years later. Before dropping out, he had failed to improve on fifth position from the season opener in South Africa.

As for Fittipaldi, he made his debut in Great Britain with an eighth position and came close to the podium finishing fourth in the next race, Germany. After Rindt's death, he returned to the tracks in the

United States achieving an authoritative victory that gave him his first win in his first season in the competition. The great promise had a total of 12 points in five races, finishing tenth in the drivers' standings.

The Swede Reine Wissell contested the last two races of the season, debuting in Formula 1 with a podium finish after finishing third in the United States.

As a team, in the latter part of the season Lotus suffered the loss of Rindt, as Ferrari won three of the four remaining rounds following the Austrian's death. However, Fittipaldi's victory, breaking the Italian team's streak, was key so that Lotus could finally maintain first position and win its fourth constructors' championship with a 7-point lead over Ferrari.

In 1971, Lotus continued to develop the successful Lotus 72 until reaching the 72D version with the collaboration of Tony Rudd, a former BRM engineer. Mainly the rear suspension and rear wing were improved to generate more downforce.

Following the unfortunate loss of Jochen Rindt, the up-and-coming Emerson Fittipaldi became the team's main driver. Reine Wissell, who had made her debut with a podium at the end of the season, got a complete program for this new edition.

[34]

[34]statsf1.com

As for the South African Dave Charlton, he would participate in the races in the Netherlands and Great Britain, although he would not manage to cross the finish line in any of them.

The season started with a fourth place for Reine Wisell in the first race in South Africa with Fittipaldi retiring.

In the second race in Spain, it was the two who failed to finish the race, and in the third in Monaco the results were reversed: Fittipaldi was fifth and Wisell retired.

With a rather mediocre start, improvements to the Lotus 72 improved results in the middle part of the season. In the four races in France, Great Britain, Germany and Austria, Fittipaldi managed to get on the podium three times.

Wisell finished in the top ten in three of them. In this way, the team returned to the podium and to frequently score points... but winning a race again became a very difficult objective.

35

[35]pinterest.es

The final part of the season did not improve, and both Fittipaldi and Wisell managed to finish in the top ten, but another podium was not achieved again, which considering that Lotus was the reigning champion, were rather poor results than , once again, led to a negative trend after having achieved a championship.

Fittipaldi finished sixth in the drivers' standings with 16 points, while Reine Wissell finished 12th with nine points. Overall, the manufacturer fell to fifth position, with no chance of retaining the world title that went to Tyrrell.

Despite this, the now renamed John Player Team Lotus (who changed the color red for the combination of black and gold), continued to trust the Lotus 72D and the possibilities of Emerson Fittipaldi as main driver.

The Swede Reine Wissell, although he would return for the last two races, was replaced throughout the year by David Walker. The Australian had already driven for Lotus the previous year, to test the experimental Pratt & Whitney turbine-powered Lotus 56B. He had participated in the Dutch race, taking advantage of the rain to gain 10 positions in the race, although he finally had to retire.

36

[36]wikiwand.com

With a car practically identical to that of the previous season in which great results had not been achieved, the Lotus team had before it a great challenge for the year 1972.

With Fittipaldi withdrawing with suspension problems and Walker being disqualified for receiving outside help, the season did not start well at the Argentine premiere.

However, everything changed from the second event in South Africa, where Fittipaldi was able to lead the race until lap 56 where he lost the lead against Denny Hulme's McLaren. Fittipaldi finished second, a good result that encouraged the team to continue improving.

In fact, it was the first of six consecutive races in which Fittipaldi did not get off the podium. And not only that, but he won three of them: Spain, Belgium and Great Britain. In France he was second and in Monaco third.

37

This good run was only interrupted by retirement in Germany due to a broken gearbox. The German test was followed by two more victories, Austria and Italy, with the Brazilian reaching his full potential and showing what an excellent driver he had become.

The last two races weren't so beneficial, with an eleventh position in Canada and retiring in the United States... but by then, the Brazilian had already scored the necessary points so that despite the last two bad results, no one would threaten his first position in the pilot classification. In this way, without any opposition, with Jackie Stewart and Denny Hulme more than 15 points behind him, Emerson Fittipaldi managed to win his first world championship. The Brazilian promise became the youngest champion in the history of the competition at 25 years, 8 months and nine days.

38

[38]lotustalk.com

David Walker did not have such a prosperous season. After finishing tenth in South Africa and ninth in Spain earlier in the season, he never finished in the top ten again, finishing the year without a point.

Reine Wissell, after participating with BRM (withdrawn in all races), returned to Lotus for the last three rounds, finishing 12th in Italy, retiring in Canada and 10th in the United States.

Luckily for Lotus, Fittipaldi's absolute dominance allowed the manufacturer to reach the top position without much suffering, despite the push from Stewart's Tyrrell, who, although he won the last two races, was not enough to jeopardize the fifth world championship. of Lotus Builders.

In 1973 John Player Team Lotus continued to rely on the Lotus 72, with minor tweaks to become the 72E, confident that the car would still suffice in the hands of a champion like Emerson Fittipaldi. This new version was adapted to the new regulations that forced the use of a deformable structure, which generated a more robust single-seater.

The Brazilian was accompanied this time by the Swede Ronnie Peterson, in a year in which Lotus chose to use only two drivers in its squad.

Peterson had made his Formula 1 debut three years earlier, driving Antique Automobiles and Colin Crabbe in his first season.

The next two years he drove for the STP March Racing Team, where in his first year he scored five podium finishes to become runner-up.

The second year with March was not as prolific, with a lone podium finish and a drop to ninth in the drivers' position.

Now, with a winning team like Lotus, he hoped to not only achieve his first victory, but even aspire to challenge for the championship.

Fittipaldi started the season the same way he finished the previous one: dominating the competition. In the first six races, he did not get off the podium, winning the races in Argentina, Brazil and Spain. In that period of time, Peterson racked up four DNFs, which he made up for by finishing on the podium in Monaco.

Despite Fittipaldi's dominance, Jackie Stewart was not willing to let himself be beaten easily this time, and of those first six races, he won all those in which the Brazilian was not a winner.

The middle part of the championship was disastrous for Fittipaldi, who, after finishing 12th in Sweden, suffered three consecutive retirements. Instead, Peterson saw his performance improve, finishing in the top three in three of those four races, and even taking victory, the first of his career, in France.

Fortunately, the middle part of the championship was not very prosperous for Stewart either, who also had problems to finish on the podium.

However, in the particular fight between the two, the Briton recovered earlier, starting the last third of the season with two victories in Holland and Germany.

Fittipaldi began to distance himself too much in the classification table, and also could not find victory again, even though he finished second in Italy and Canada, so he finally reached the last event in the United States without any option to fight for the championship against Stewart, having to settle for the second position.

As for Peterson, he continued his adaptation and progress throughout the year, and despite the poor start to the season, he has won three of the last four races (Austria, Italy and the United States). This allowed him to finish third in the drivers' championship, just three points behind his teammate Fittipaldi. If he hadn't suffered so many reliability problems in the early part of the season, he could have aspired to much more.

---

[40]deviantart.com

With the good performance of its two drivers, where one was able to achieve victories when the other was not enjoying his best moment, 7 victories were achieved out of the 15 total races and Lotus was at least able to win the constructors' championship again, adding their sixth world title as a team.

For the 1974 season, the new Lotus 76 was planned to be released, an improved version of the Lotus 72 with less weight and narrower, but which was not at all convincing, forcing us to use the Lotus 72 once again, this time evolved into its version 72E.

However, who would no longer be in the team would be Emerson Fittipaldi, who signed for McLaren to drive an M23 very similar to the Lotus.

The Brazilian star was replaced at John Player Team Lotus by Jacky Ickx. The Belgian had already accumulated experience in Formula 1 since he debuted in 1966 with the Tyrrell Racing Organization, a team with which he only participated in Germany for two years in the Formula 2 category, retiring in both races. In 1967, he also drove for the Cooper Car Company in two races, earning his first point at Monza.

A year later, he achieved his first full participation with Ferrari, achieving his first victory in France to which he added three more podiums to finish fourth in the final drivers' standings.

After passing through Motor Racing Developments Ltd where he added two more victories becoming runner-up, he returned to Ferrari in a new stage of four years of association with the legendary Italian team, where after another runner-up in 1970, he finished fourth in the standings in the two following years.

In 1973, his last year at Ferrari, he did not achieve a podium finish throughout the campaign, which meant that he ended the year driving for McLaren and Williams, in what was already confirmed as the end of his relationship with Ferrari.

Now, with Lotus, he was confident of getting back on the road to victories and fighting for that world championship that had narrowly eluded him on two occasions.

41

The season started with serious reliability problems, with Peterson retiring in three of the first five races, and Ickx having to retire in six of the first seven events.

At least Peterson was victorious in Monaco, the sixth round of the championship, and Jacky had managed to get on the podium in Brazil in the only race he had managed to finish in the first part of the competition.

---

[41]aminoapps.com

The middle part of the championship improved for Lotus, with Peterson achieving another victory in France and another in Italy, and Jacky Ickx once again getting on the podium in Great Britain, but the mechanical problems were always present and did not give the impression throughout the whole year that Lotus could fight to win the championship. Peterson had finally managed to win three races throughout the season, the same as Fittipaldi with his new McLaren, but the difference in consistency meant that the Swede finished fifth in the final drivers' standings, while his former teammate won a new McLaren championship. world (after an even fight with Regazzoni's Ferrari).

As for the constructors' standings, despite Peterson's efforts, Lotus dropped to fourth position, this time surpassed by McLaren, Ferrari and Tyrrell. Once again, Lotus demonstrated its difficulties to stay at the top once it had won the championship.

The 1975 season threatened to be a replica of the previous campaign, again using the Lotus 72 which, despite its new suspension, was clearly becoming outdated and incapable of competing with other top brands.

Peterson and Jackie Ickx also repeated as team drivers, in what was a completely continuous campaign with the previous one.

As expected, the results continued their negative trend. Peterson was once again the best driver in the team, but this time he failed to get on the podium in any of the fourteen races.

43

His best finish was a fourth position in Monaco. He finished fifth in Austria and the United States and ninth in Sweden, and the rest of the races he could not finish higher than 10th, which saw him finish 13th in the drivers' championship with just 6 points. Jacky Ickx did manage to climb to the podium with a second position in the tragic race in Spain that had to be interrupted, but the rest of the races he managed with difficulties to finish in the top ten. Desperate, he quit the team and the competition with five races to go.

For the final part, Ickx was replaced by the British Jim Crawford, John Watson and Brian Henton, but none of them managed to score any more points for the Lotus team, which fell to seventh position, concluding its gradual decline.

In 1976, the successful Lotus 72 was finally abandoned and replaced by the new Lotus 77 with the hope of ending the team's negative trend. The Lotus 77 completed the failed idea of the Lotus 76, that is, it achieved a lighter car to make the most of the power of the DFV Cosworth.

Instead of wishbones, the suspension was based on rockers. Radiators were repositioned to improve cooling, and aerodynamics were improved over its predecessor.

The car had to receive many improvements throughout the year, especially at the suspension level, hiring engineers such as Len Terry or Tony Southgate for this.

Despite the efforts, all the drivers agreed that it was an unwieldy vehicle, that it did not respond properly, and that it was also slow on the straights.

44

Ronnie Peterson was to be the hope of Lotus again, but after his accidental retirement in the first race in Brazil, he decided to continue the season at March Engineering. Lotus had to turn to his compatriot Gunnar Nilsson, who was making his Formula 1 debut after winning the British Formula 3 Championship.

The second new driver for the team was the American Mario Andretti (although he would be replaced by Bob Evans in two races). Andretti had already driven punctually for Lotus in 1968 and 1969 (without managing to finish any race). In 1970 he drove for STP Corporation, where he participated in four races, abandoning in three, but achieving the podium in Spain in which he was able to finish.

After that he spent two years at Ferrari, where he achieved his first victory in South Africa. With Vel's Parnelli Jones Racing team he got his first complete program in 1965, adding 5 points to finish 14th in the final standings.

Now, with more experience in the competition, he returned to Lotus looking to add more victories to his career.

---

[45]Fanat1cos.com

The new Lotus 77, in addition to being unwieldy, proved to be a very fragile single-seater. Andretti suffered eight retirements throughout the season and Nilsson nine.

The reliability problems were progressively resolved, and at least by the end of the season the Lotus 77 began to be competitive with the improvements, especially in the hands of Andretti, who was able to close the season with a victory at the Japanese Grand Prix. In the last part of the season, he had also managed to get podium finishes in the Netherlands and Canada to move up to the sixth final position in the drivers' championship.

As for Nilsson, he was able to add two podium finishes repeating third position in Austria and Spain, finally adding 10 points that took him to the final tenth place.

---

[46]britannica.com

Lotus ended up in fourth position in the constructors' championship, still far from regaining glory, but at least it put an end to the negative trend, managed to win a race again and, above all, with the improvement in performance in the final part of the season, hope was restored.

Aware of the problems of the Lotus 77, the Lotus 78 was developed for the 1977 season. The Lotus 78, designed by Colin Chapman, Peter Wright, Tony Rudd and Martin Ogilvie, would revolutionize Formula 1.

Colin Chapman, in a new demonstration of his brilliant ability as an engineer, ended up incorporating ground effect in Formula 1 single-seaters with the Lotus 78.

He had noticed how the airflow across the wings of airplanes worked to get them to lift and stay airborne, and he had thought that doing the reverse effect might be beneficial for a racing car.

After extensive experimentation with inverted wings, various car backgrounds and a wind tunnel, the development team came to a conclusion: as the vehicle increased its speed, its surface moved closer to the ground. After innumerable tests with cardboard models, an adequate configuration between chassis and wings was achieved to enhance the so-called "ground effect".

Ground effect takes advantage of the airflow under the car and redirects it to the rear wing to "glue" the car to the asphalt. In this way, extra thrust is achieved and it is possible to face the corners at higher speed without the car ending up leaving the track and staying locked to the trajectory even at higher speeds.

The Lotus 78 was finally the result of the basic structure of the successful Lotus 72, with the improvements in terms of weight reduction of the Lotus 77 (now also using lighter materials such as aluminum), in combination with the newly discovered aerodynamic elements. In this way, Chapman's team had succeeded in creating an engineering marvel.

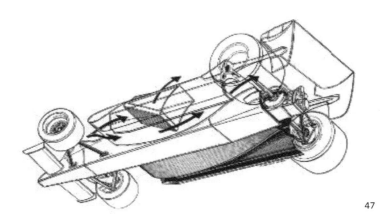

Mario Andretti and Gunnar Nilsson repeated as drivers to start driving this new and promising Lotus 78.

Despite the revolution that the new car represented, the first results were not excellent, with a fifth position as the best result in the first three races (Andretti in Argentina and Nilsson in Brazil).

However, immediately afterward the victories began to come. Mario Andretti had two consecutive victories in the United States West and in Spain and Nilsson achieved victory in Belgium. Andretti won again in France to close out a first half of the season with four wins.

---

[47]aerodynamicaf1.com

48

The second part of the season began with a double DNF in three consecutive races (Germany, Austria and the Netherlands) that weighed down the entire campaign. Andretti would win again in Italy and be second in the United States of the East, but Gunnar Nilsson would end up retiring in all races accumulating seven consecutive DNFs.

These results completed a year of ups and downs, with frequent successes but with reliability problems also very present on many occasions. Andretti was third in the final drivers' standings, 25 points behind champion Niki Lauda, and Nilsson was eighth.

Overall, Lotus beat McLaren in their personal fight for the constructors' runner-up, but was more than 30 points behind the champion of the edition: Ferrari. Even so, a new hope had been

---

[48]elsofadelaf1.blogspot.com

created, and if the mistakes of the early phase of a new project could be corrected, the Lotus 78 could lead the team once again to fight for the championship.

In this way, the Lotus 79 was a refined version of the Lotus 78, trying to improve the problems that its predecessor had shown, such as the problematic airflow through the rear suspension that caused some understeer and low pressure in the front area. of the car, which forced the use of a very large wing which, due to the high resistance, decreased the maximum speed, a problem they had suffered in the previous season on the fastest circuits.

This time, Ronnie Peterson returned to John Player Team Lotus in exchange for his teammate Gunnar Nilsson, to form, together with Mario Andretti, the team's official driver squad.

With this new improved version of the ground effect Lotus, Andretti this time started the season by winning the opening round in Argentina.

[49]

[49]formulaonestuff.com

In the third test in South Africa, it was Peterson who claimed victory. Meanwhile, Carlos Reutemann became Lotus' main rival with his Ferrari.

In the middle part of the championship, the Lotus 78 began to be invincible, with the entire grid wondering what could be the secret of the car, a secret that it hid in its bottom and its modifications to redirect the airflow.

In Belgium, France, Spain and the Netherlands, Lotus achieved four doubles, with Andretti always ahead of Peterson, the Lotus taking the first two positions at the end of the races.

In Germany the doublet could not be repeated due to Peterson's abandonment, but Andretti won the event, the opposite occurring in Austria.

In total, and with three races to go, Lotus had achieved 8 victories out of a possible 13, with Reutemann's Ferrari and Niki Lauda's Brabham dividing up the victories that Lotus let slip away (with the exception of Patrick Depailler's victory in Monaco).

In this way, Andretti arrived in Italy, the penultimate round of the championship, with 63 points, while his teammate Peterson accumulated 51 points, well above the 35 points of Niki Lauda in third position.

However, despite the joy and optimism in the team, Monza turned out to be a fateful grand prix for Lotus.

The light turned green before all the cars were in their starting positions, so some cars that were still moving had an advantage over those that were stationary.

This created a mess that intensified on arrival at the first chicane which left little room to manoeuvre.

James Hunt turned left as Riccardo Patrese came towards him with great speed to avoid him, hitting the rear wheel of Peterson's Lotus, which ended up crashing into the barriers.

Peterson's car caught fire, but the Swedish driver was able to get out with the help of Hunt, Depailler and Regazzoni before suffering more serious burns, and after 20 endless minutes the medical services came to take him to hospital.

50

At the Milan hospital, the tests showed that Ronnie had 17 fractures in one leg and 3 in the other, which ended up becoming complicated, generating a fat embolism that caused multiple organ failure that ended his life. Thus, one of the most talented drivers in the history of Formula 1 lost his life.

51

For the last two races of the season, Peterson was replaced by Frenchman Jean-Pierre Jarier, who had driven since 1974 for Shadow, achieving a podium finish in Monaco that same year for his best result (his best placing in a final drivers' standings had been 14th).

Jarier finished 15th in the United States and ended up dropping out in Canada. Nor did Andretti have a good end to the season, with the entire Lotus team affected after the loss of Peterson. The American had to retire in his own country and finished tenth in the last race in Canada.

Late in the season, Reutemann and Niki Lauda continued to score victories, but Andretti had already built enough of a lead to secure first place and claim world champion.

52

In fact, the fight between Reuteman and Lauda focused more on snatching the runner-up from the late Ronnie Peterson. Reutemann and Lauda had the option of taking second place in the last race, but the Austrian retired with brake problems while the Argentine, who needed to win the race, finished in third position.

In this way, Ronnie Peterson achieved the runner-up posthumously.

As it could not be otherwise, with its two drivers in the first two positions in the final standings, Lotus won its seventh world championship for constructors, with a considerable advantage of 28 points over Ferrari.

For the 1979 season, John Player disappeared from Formula 1 and Lotus opted for Martini as main sponsor, renaming itself Martini Racing Team Lotus and acquiring a dark green coloration.

Unknowingly, Lotus began a new stage in his career, leaving behind the classic black and gold John Player Lotus.

The team was still confident in the absolute superiority of its ground effect Lotus 79 for this new year. However, his secret was discovered and very soon the rest of the grid began to copy his innovations, losing the advantage obtained.

To counter this, Lotus brought in the Lotus 80 from the fifth race onwards looking to stay one step ahead of the rest again. The objective of the Lotus 80 was to extend the ground effect under the nose, to spread the airflow and to convert practically the entire lower part of the car into a ground effect generator trying to enhance the effect that had allowed them to win the championship the previous season. .

An improved aerodynamic effect was achieved, but paradoxically, this ruined the car's chances. By getting so much downforce, under braking there was such a drop in downforce that the car seemed to rise and fall and it became very difficult to drive in slow corners.

---

[53]pinterest.es

To replace Peterson, the team signed Carlos Reutemann as Andretti's teammate.

Because of this, the Lotus 80 was driven in only four races by Mario Andretti, before returning to the previous Lotus 79. The Argentine had made his Formula 1 debut in 1972, driving three years for Motor Racing Developments achieving two podium finishes in the second year. with the team and three victories in the third. In 1975, he signed for Martini Racing, where he continued to win to finish fourth in the final drivers' standings.

1976 was not such a prosperous year for him with Martini Racing, with numerous retirements and a fourth position in Spain as his best result, ending the year driving for Ferrari in Italy.

Reutemann convinced the legendary Italian team, since the following two years he drove for Ferrari, adding five more victories to his record, and being the driver who gave the insurmountable Lotus the most problems in 1978.

54

In this way, Lotus got the two drivers best positioned in the previous season's standings (not counting Peterson), and together with a car that seemed invincible, the objective was none other than to win the championship again.

Reutemann opened with a second place in the opening test in Argentina, and repeated the podium in the second test in Brazil. He was again on the podium in Spain along with his teammate Andretti's first podium finish in the fifth event of the season.

55

Despite the fact that the two Lotuses managed to get on the podium in the Spanish event, the feelings were negative. It was evident that a winning car was no longer available and that the other teams had already made good use of ground effect.

[55]Izquierdadiario.es

The results did not improve throughout the year, not even with the arrival of the Lotus 80 whose withdrawal put an end to hopes of improvement in the second half of the season.

In fact, Reutemann's third position in Monaco, the seventh event of the season, was the last podium for Lotus throughout the year. The second half of the year was disastrous, with numerous retirements and a fifth position for Andretti in Italy as the only points scored in the second part of the season.

In this way, Carlos Reutemann finished seventh in the final drivers' classification and Mario Andretti 12th. In a disappointing campaign, Lotus saw Ferrari, Williams and Ligier easily overtake them in the final manufacturers' standings.

Once again, Lotus could not retain the glory once achieved, and ended a year that meant descending from paradise to a sad reality.

The 80s and the search for past glory with Elio de Angelis, Nigel Mansell and Ayrton Senna

Following the disappointment of 1979, Lotus was dropping Martini as a major partner and partnering with Essex to kick off the new decade. With the innovative ground effect implemented by virtually the entire grid, it was clear that a new car was needed, and for 1980 the team relied on the Lotus 81.

The lack of involvement of Colin Chapman in the development meant that the new car was less innovative, with very standard features, with the sliding skirts and the bottom that many other vehicles already used.

56

Mario Andretti continued as the main driver of a squad that was joined by Elio de Angelis.

The Italian had debuted in Formula 1 the previous season after being Italian Formula 3 champion in 1977 and winning the Monaco Formula 2 Grand Prix in 1978.

In 1979 he drove for the Interscope Shadow Racing team where he regularly finished races between seventh and 12th. In the last Grand Prix, in the United States, he achieved his best result by finishing in fourth position, adding the first points of his career.

[56]retroracecars.com

The Lotus 81 debuted with a double DNF in Argentina, but in the next race Elio de Angelis achieved a magnificent second position in Brazil, only being surpassed by René Arnoux's Renault.

However, Elio's podium finish was only a glimpse of what the season would turn out to be. The Italian did not get on the podium again all year, and Andretti underperformed, failing to score points until the last race in the United States where, with a sixth position, he collected his only point of the season.

The team's poor performance was also due to numerous reliability issues, racking up a large number of retirements. Even getting John Player back as a sponsor by trying to conjure up past glory from the fifth race onwards didn't help avoid another disappointing season.

Elio de Angelis finished seventh in the final standings, getting 13 points, while Andretti finished in 20th position.

Late in the season, Lotus also brought in a rookie Nigel Mansell for

---

the races in Austria, the Netherlands and Italy. Despite the difficult stage of the Englishman in Formula 3, including the serious accident with Andrea de Cesaris that crushed a vertebra (and after which the doctors assured him that he would not drive again), Colin Chapman noticed him and offered proof. After performing it with painkillers to avoid the pain of his injuries, Chapman hired him as a test pilot. At the end of 1980, he finally had the opportunity to debut in Formula 1, although he could not finish the races in Austria and the Netherlands and for Italy he did not even qualify.

58

As a team, Lotus finished fifth, behind Williams, Ligier, Brabham and Renault. The only consolation was that the few points that Elio de Angelis had collected had come in the final stretch of the season. With the exception of his podium in Brazil, the rest of the points had been gained in the last five races. This indicated that the team had progressed throughout the year and gave hope for the new season.

This season began with the Lotus 81 with the expectation of incorporating the revolutionary double chassis Lotus 88. The innovation of this single-seater consisted of a chassis to compensate the internal mechanical forces of the car itself and another to take advantage of the aerodynamic force coming from the outside. As speed increased, the outer chassis lowered onto the inner one, increasing downforce.

[59]

This design was banned by the FIA due to the rule that prevented the use of movable aerodynamic elements. This prohibition generated some controversy, since the rule prevented the use of aerodynamic elements attached to moving parts of the car, but Lotus claimed that it was not an additional element, but the chassis itself.

In any case, Lotus was forced to complete the season with the Lotus 87, a more traditional version that incorporated a single carbon fiber chassis, being one of the first vehicles to use this material along with McLaren.

---

[59]statsf1.com

Elio de Angelis continued as the team's starting driver, while Andretti, after a year of poor performance, finally left the team to join Alfa Romeo. His place was taken by Nigel Mansell, who despite not having shone in his three opportunities the previous season, maintained the confidence of Chapman, who had managed to see in him the future champion he would become.

In the first races, still with the Lotus from the previous year, Elio de Angelis managed to score points in Brazil and Argentina. It was expected to improve the results with the new Lotus 88 that was finally banned, so the team had to participate from the fifth race with the Lotus 87.

The results did not improve. Elio de Angelis managed to continue scoring frequently. In fact, not counting his two retirements and the disqualification in Great Britain, he always finished seventh or better.

---

[60]ultimatecarpage.com

But he did not achieve the performance necessary to get on the podium throughout the year. Finally, he finished eighth with 14 points.

As for Nigel Mansell, he did manage to get on the podium in Belgium, but he was the exception to a generally difficult year, managing only points in Spain and the United States, and retiring eight times. Despite putting Lotus back on the podium, he finished 14th with eight points.

In a difficult new year, Lotus slipped to seventh in the manufacturers' final position, in a year in which the regulations had frustrated Chapman's creative efforts.

For the 1982 season, Lotus developed the Lotus 91 hoping to have fewer problems with their new car than the previous season. To do this, the team formed by Colin Chapman, Martin Ogilvie and Tony Rudd sought a more traditional concept, after recent disappointments with the more experimental versions.

The use of carbon fiber and kevlar was expanded with the intention of making a lighter car, since the DFV Cosworth engine began to show less power compared to the new turbocharged engines. With a lighter weight, they hoped to make better use of the now limited power of the engine that had become the most successful in Formula 1 history.

The sidepods were turned into complete pieces to the rear looking to take even more advantage of ground effect.

61

Elio de Angelis was once again the most consistent driver throughout the season, with a similar performance to the previous season. The Italian managed to score points with great frequency, but the podium eluded him despite taking fourth place in Belgium, Canada and Great Britain.

The highlight of the Italian's season came in Austria, where he competed for victory against Keke Rosberg's almighty Williams right to the end, in a battle so close that Elio de Angelis finally claimed his first victory just five hundredths ahead of his rival. Although Lotus did not give the impression that they could regularly stay at the top of Formula 1 again, at least they managed to get another victory.

[61]ultimatecarpage.com

62

With this victory, Elio de Angelis had a total of 23 points to finish ninth in the final standings.

As for Nigel Mansell, his performance was similar to the previous year. He got another podium by finishing third in Brazil, but the rest of the year, while he often managed to finish in the top ten, he only returned to points in Monaco finishing fourth. In total, he added 7 points finishing 14th.

As a team, Lotus moved up slightly to fifth position behind Ferrari, McLaren, Renault and Williams, but coming back to victory again was an important dose of excitement to keep working.

However, in December of that year Lotus received the worst news. Colin Chapman died suddenly of heart failure, thus losing the founder of the team and one of the most brilliant and creative engineers in the competition.

---

[62]Motor.es

63

After Chapman's death, the team was led by Peter Eric Warr, a businessman and former driver, who had already led Formula 1 teams such as Walter Wolf Racing or Fittipaldi Automotive. Peter Warr had previously worked with Lotus, acting as manager during the heyday that saw Jochen Rindt and Emerson Fittipaldi become champions.

Despite Chapman's death, his spirit still remained in the 1983 Lotus 92, the last single-seater in which he was involved in its development. This vehicle was characterized by introducing the active suspension in the competition.

This revolutionary system allowed the height and behavior of the suspension to be modified from the cabin through valves (later it would be electronically controlled by computers).

This allowed the car's suspension to be adjusted to the different

---

[63] quadis.es

characteristics of the layout along its length, optimizing it according to certain parts of the circuit.

In addition to the active suspension, the Lotus 92 incorporated the new Cosworth DFY V8 engine, an evolution of the successful DFV Cosworth that had become obsolete with the arrival of the turbo in Formula 1 incorporated by Renault. It was also the last car to feature a non-turbo engine until the subsequent ban on this item in 1989.

[64]

This car was only used for 8 races, and only by Nigel Mansell (except for the first race where it was also used by Elio de Angelis). This model only managed to score once with a sixth position from Mansell in Germany.

Aware that the turbo was no longer an advantage, but a necessity, Chapman had also considered making an alternative model that abandoned its long relationship with Cosworth engines, so this year the Lotus 93T was also used.

---

[64]gasolinesuper.es

The Lotus 93T was a version of the Lotus 92 adapted to the Renault-Gordini EF1 1.5 V6t engines, which already incorporated the new turbocharging system. Due to its reliability problems, the single-seater ended up being revised to give rise to its 94T version.

65

Elio de Angelis has driven this car since the second race of the year, which was characterized by reliability problems. The Italian had to retire in twelve races, being able to finish in Belgium finishing in ninth position and in Italy in fifth position, getting his only two points of the season.

Mansell's switch to the turbocharged Lotus 93 mid-season did bring a performance upgrade for him, scoring points more often with a fourth in Great Britain and fifth in Austria. Despite also suffering from reliability problems, he even managed to get on the podium at the European Grand Prix. For the first time, Mansell surpassed his teammate in the classification, although he finished 13th compared to the eighteenth position of Elio de Angelis.

In a year dominated by mechanical problems, Lotus-Renault finished in eighth place in the manufacturers with 11 points, well ahead of Lotus-Ford which had only added one point. In this complicated way, Lotus entered the turbo era.

For the 1984 season, the new Lotus 95T featured a new Renault engine, the EF4B 1.5 V6t, in the hope that reliability issues would be ameliorated. It was an evolved version of its predecessor, adapted to Goodyear tires, after leaving Pirelli.

66

[66]pinterest.es

The season began with a podium finish for Elio de Angelis, finishing third in Brazil, a position he repeated three races later in San Marino. The next three races he continued to score points to return to the podium in both races in the United States. In this way, the Italian completed a satisfactory first half of the championship, finishing almost all the races at the top of the standings.

In the last seven races he did not get on the podium again, with mechanical problems that made him abandon in half the dates. At least, the races that he managed to finish, he finished in the points zone. This allowed him a remarkable regularity to accumulate 34 points and, despite not winning any race, he managed to finish in a creditable third final position in the drivers' championship, although well behind the tight duel between Niki Lauda and Alain Prost, with both exceeding 70 points.

Meanwhile, Mansell began the season with four DNFs to later climb to the podium in France. This dynamic was maintained for the rest of the year. Like his teammate, he retired in half the races, but in the other half he managed to score points, as well as adding another podium in the Netherlands. Finally, he added 13 points to finish 10th in the final standings.

As a team, Lotus moved up to third position, behind only McLaren and Ferrari. This was a good step forward for the team in its fight to return to glory. In fact, many media claimed that the Lotus 95T was even more aerodynamically efficient than the almighty McLaren. With a few small adjustments, the return of Lotus to dominate a championship could become a reality. With this intention, the Lotus 97T was developed for the 1985 season, which would be called one of the most beautiful single-seaters in history. This was an upgraded version of the 95T, incorporating certain elements from Lotus' CART championship project, making it slightly more robust.

67

Elio de Angelis stayed with the team for another year, while Nigel Mansell finally left the team to sign for Williams.

His place was taken by Ayrton Senna. The legendary Brazilian had debuted the previous year in Formula 1 with the Toleman Group Motorsport team, a team considered to be the weakest with which he had managed to get on the podium three times (Monaco, Great Britain and Portugal), as well as scoring points in two more tests.

Lotus perceived the talent and the possible projection of the Brazilian and did not hesitate to take over his services.

The start was exciting for Lotus, with Elio de Angelis taking victory in San Marino and staying on the podium in three of the first four races.

In the second event, Ayrton Senna achieved victory in Portugal, adding the first victory of his legendary career.

After this start, there was an inauspicious five-race stretch for the team that diminished the euphoria at Lotus. Senna had to retire on three occasions and on the remaining two he could not improve from tenth position. For his part, Elio managed to score points in three of them, but did not return to the podium.

Elio de Angelis would continue this dynamic until the end of the season, suffering various retirements and finishing in fifth or sixth position in the races that he did manage to finish.

Who did have an explosion of performance was Ayrton Senna. The Brazilian finished second in Austria, the tenth round of the championship, to get on the podium for five consecutive races, in

---

one of them achieving victory in Belgium.

In the last two events, Senna ended up retiring, hampering his good season, since he could have aspired to runner-up (it was impossible to catch up to Alain Prost's dominant McLaren in qualifying). Finally, he finished in a creditable fourth position with 38 points, while Elio de Angelis was fifth with 33 points.

Lotus dropped to fourth position in the constructors' championship, one position lower than the previous season, but the sensations were even better. You had a car capable of winning races, and a driver who grew and improved race after race, with potential that seemed limitless.

The new Lotus 98T for 1986 continued the trend of previous single-seaters designed by Gérard Ducarouge and Martin Ogilvie, adapting the new car to new rules that required reducing fuel capacity to 195 litres, which resulted in a lower chassis.

Renault also improved its EF15B engine, which featured pneumatic valves for the first time.

69

After a long relationship with Lotus, Elio de Angelis left the team to start driving the Brabham of Motor Racing Developments.

Initially, the Italian was going to be replaced by Derek Warwick, in relation to an agreement with Renault. However, Ayrton Senna refused to allow the team to have two main drivers, and suggested that Mauricio Gugelmin be signed as number two.

With sponsor John Player pressing for a British driver to join the team, Johnny Dumfries was finally signed as second driver, thus making his Formula 1 debut.

70

Dumfries' lack of experience meant that the Briton had a difficult year, with a fifth position in Hungary as his best result, and only scoring points in one more event, Australia, finishing in sixth position. With just 3 points, Dumfries finished 13th in the final drivers' standings.

As for Senna, he started the season continuing his successes, with a second position in the first race in Brazil to win the next one in Spain.

Five races later he returned to victory in the United States, achieving two more podiums between one and the other. The second part of the season was somewhat more complicated, with more mechanical problems, but the Brazilian managed to score three more podiums, two of them in second position.

With 55 points, the Brazilian finished in the fourth position of drivers, only surpassed by Alain Prost, Nigel Mansell and Nelson Piquet.

Lotus moved up to third in the manufacturers' position (behind Williams and McLaren), remained at the top of the standings, and the illusion of a return to glory continued if an upward trajectory continued.

In 1987 the Colin Chapman Trophy was created in honor of the founder of Lotus, which rewarded the best team with an atmospheric engine (which ended up being Tyrrell). This mention of the man who gave rise to Lotus could be a sign of the brand's return to the top.

For this season, the Lotus 99T was developed whose main characteristic was the change from Renault engines to Honda engines, making use of the RA167E 1.5 V6t engine. This car included for the first time the electronic active suspension, so that the suspension was modified automatically through a computer, instead of having to be done manually.

The legendary John Player brand ended its relationship with Lotus, so Camel became the main sponsor, renaming the team Camel Team Lotus Honda, and using the characteristic yellow color as the vehicle's main paint.

Senna continued for another year as the team's best hope of winning championships again, and was accompanied by the Japanese Satoru Nakajima, as part of the deal with Honda for the Japanese brand to agree to supply him with its powerful engines.

In this way, Najakima debuted in Formula 1 after having been a Williams test driver for three years.

[71]soymotor.com
[72]f1.fandom.com

One more year, Ayrton Senna pushed his Lotus to the limit and had a good start to the season. Despite the retirements in Brazil and Belgium, the Brazilian managed to get on the podium in practically all the races in the first half of the season, with the exception of the French test. In Monaco and the United States, he also achieved two victories that made Lotus dream of a return to glory.

However, as had been the case for the past few years, the second part of the campaign continued on a downward trajectory in performance.

Senna was no longer able to win a race in the last eight tests. His frequency on the podium also dropped, although he managed to finish second on three more occasions: Hungary, Italy and Japan. However, this downward trend in performance prevented him from ultimately challenging for the championship, unable to keep up with Nelson Piquet's Williams who were crowned champions.

Adding to the frustration, Senna was disqualified in the final race in Australia for inadequate car dimensions, eliminating his second position which would have helped him pass Nigel Mansell in qualifying to runner-up.

For his part, Satoru Nakajima had a performance far removed from that of his partner. The Japanese did not achieve any podium, and the fourth position in Great Britain was his best result. In total, he added 7 points finishing tenth in the final standings.

Lotus was able to maintain third position in the constructors' standings, close to McLaren but a long way behind Williams. There was still just a little push left to fight for championships again, but what before was illusion and hope, not finding that extra thing the team needed, frustration began to take its toll on the team.

In 1988, the Lotus 99T was updated to the 100T version, with very small adjustments to the front and rear of the chassis, being practically the same single-seater.

However, this time the talented Ayrton Senna would no longer be there to drive it. The Brazilian signed for McLaren, looking for that winning car at the height of his capabilities that he seemed not to find in Lotus year after year.

Senna was replaced by his compatriot Nelson Piquet, the defending champion after having managed to win the championship the previous season. In addition, he had also been champion in 1981 and 1983 with the Brabham of Parmalat Racing Team and Fila Sport. Therefore, Lotus lost Senna but got the services of a three-time champion in top form, hoping that this time it would be enough to win a title.

73

Piquet started with two hopeful podiums in the first two races in Brazil and San Marino, but the hope of improving to win soon turned into the satisfaction of getting another podium again.

The few updates to the Lotus 100T were not enough to take advantage of the Brazilian's talent, and although he usually finished races in the top positions, he only got one more podium again in the last race in Australia, adding 22 points and settling for a sixth position in a year in which McLaren dominated at will with Ayrton Senna and Alain Prost.

74

As for Nakajima, he once again completed a very discreet season, with a sixth position in Brazil as his best result, adding a single point throughout the year.

---

[74]deviantart.com

With this, Lotus dropped to fourth position in the constructors' championship behind McLaren, Ferrari and Benetton, and took a step back.

After the failure of the Lotus 100T, Ducarouge left Lotus and development of the new Lotus 101 was carried out by Frank Dernie, a former Williams aerodynamic engineer. However, the addition of Dernie was made late, with the car already practically developed by Mike Coughlan.

With turbo banned, Lotus turned to Judd's naturally aspirated 1.5-litre V8 engines, so the aim of the new cars was to try to make up for the lack of power after the ban on turbocharging. To achieve this, Lotus relied on getting a much lighter car, so much so that due to the small cabin, a special steering wheel had to be developed to accommodate the pilots.

75

It soon became clear that the new Lotus meant another step backwards for the team, this time unable to even achieve a podium finish in the first part of the championship (although Piquet was on the verge of achieving it with fourth position in Canada and Great Britain).

In addition, as usual when new engines were incorporated, reliability problems were numerous.

Lotus's problems were the low capacity of its new engine (which generated 80 horsepower less than the Honda engine used by McLaren) and the difficulty of heating the Goodyear tires, designed for more robust cars to have more power like the McLarens. Or the Ferraris.

The poor results caused the Chapman family, who held shares in the team, to pressure Peter Warr to leave the team, which became managed by Tony Rudd.

The arrival of Rudd could not change the dynamics in the second half of the season, which continued without any podium finishes, with Piquet settling again closing in on him, scoring points in three more races to get a total of 12 points that saw him finish in the eighth position.

Nakajima, for his part, only managed to score points in Australia, sending the Lotus down to sixth in a negative momentum that threatened to continue an unstoppable free fall.

The 1990s and the decline of Lotus

The new decade began with a Lotus team in regression, filled with uncertainty and with hopes of another Formula 1 success fading.

Furthermore, both Nelson Piquet and Satoru Nakajima left the team, forcing Lotus to start from scratch and restart a new cycle.

Camel Team Lotus ditched Judd engines and this time relied on the Lamborghini 3512 3.5 for the Lotus 102, making it the only V12-powered car.

With more involvement from Frank Dernie this time, the Lotus 102 ended up being a robust and heavy car. The new regulations allowed larger fuel tanks, which together with the heavy Lamborghini engine increased the final weight of the vehicle. The team was confident that the power from the new engine would be sufficient so that weight would not be an issue.

For the new squad, Lotus had two British drivers. The first of them was Derek Warwick, a driver who had made his debut in Formula 1 with Toleman in 1981, a year in which he only managed to qualify for one of the 12 races in which he participated, and which he also ended up abandoning.

The next two years with Toleman were better, scoring points in the last four races of 1983. After that, he spent two years with Renault where he scored his first podium finishes before driving for Brabham in 1986 in a season that marked a step back in his career. without getting any points.

---

[76]pinterest.es

The next three years he drove for Arrows, often finishing in the points zone, and with his move to Lotus he was confident he could return to the podium.

The second driver was Martin Donelly, who had been a Lotus test driver since 1988. In 1989, he had replaced Warwick at Arrows for the French event after damaging his back in a karting race, finishing in twelfth position. This year, he became the starting driver alongside the man he had replaced last season.

---

[77]museonicolis.com

The season began with double DNFs in the first two races in the United States and Brazil. DNFs were frequent throughout the season (the team suffered up to six more double DNFs), and the races that did manage to finish both drivers tended to finish in the top ten positions, but rarely within the points.

Only Warwick was able to score points with a sixth position in Canada and a fifth position in Hungary, adding the only three points that led Lotus to fall to the final eighth position in the constructors' world championship, aggravating its negative trend.

Donnelly suffered a serious accident at the Spanish Grand Prix, being thrown from the car (with the seat included), thus ending his career in Formula 1.

He was replaced for the last two races by Johnny Herbert, who had made his debut in the competition the previous season with Benetton scoring points in two of the six races with the team, and also participating with Tyrrell on two occasions retiring in one race and failing to qualify for the other. In Lotus, with the fragility of the

---

[78]f1.fandom.com

Lotus 102, he could not finish the race in his two participations either.

In 1991, the relationship with Camel ended, so the team returned to its original name long before the arrival of sponsors in Formula 1: Team Lotus.

With the aim of ending the team's dangerous negative trend, numerous new elements were used for the car, but the final result was not very different from the Lotus 102 of the previous season, so it ended up being renamed the Lotus 102B, whose larger The difference with its predecessor was the loss of Camel's own striking yellow color to adopt a mainly white coloration with dark green.

This year they also turned to Judd engines, using the EV 3.5 V8, ditching the Lamborghini engine. The driver squad was also completely revamped, in a clear sign that Lotus was trying to change as much as possible to improve its results, but the result seemed more like a haphazard attempt to find a solution without knowing exactly what to fix.

Mika Häkkinen joined the team after a successful initial stage in karting and winning the Formula Opel Euroseries in 1988 and the British Formula 3 in 1990. The Finn thus began his career in Formula 1 at the hands of Lotus.

---

[79]F1forever.wordpress.com

80

Häkkinen's teammate was Julian Bailey, at least for the first four races of the season, as the second car would end up being driven by as many as three different drivers throughout the year.

Bailey had only driven in the 1988 edition of Formula 1 with the Tyrrell Racing Organization team, failing to qualify for the race in half of the season's events.

81

---

[80]Pilotoshistoricos.blogspot.com
[81]Fiaresultsandstatistics.motorsportstats.com

With a car very similar to that of the previous season and two drivers with little experience in competition, expectations were not favorable for Lotus.

In his four races with the team, Julian Bailey managed to score points with his sixth position in Monaco, but the rest of the races he failed to qualify, which was a grievance for Lotus, which went from being a historically champion team to not achieving the necessary performance. to participate in the races.

For this reason, Bailey was fired and replaced by Johnny Herbert, who had already participated with the team in the last two races of the previous season. Herbert also failed to qualify in his first appearance in Canada, but the next two races he managed to finish in tenth position.

Even so, the results were not good and four races later Lotus replaced him with the German Michael Bartels, who had managed to finish in the top positions in the different national championships, although without winning any of them.

Bartels and Herbert ended up alternating in the second car for the rest of the season. While the German failed to qualify in any of his four Lotus outings, Herbert did manage to finish around tenth in five of them, but neither man scored any points.

Meanwhile, Häkkinen was at least giving the team some hope with the other car. The Finn scored the first points for the team in the third race with his fifth position in San Marino. However, these were the only points for Häkkinen and for Lotus throughout the season. Although the Finn managed to qualify for all the races except one, he finished them in the final part of the classification. Not even the arrival of sponsors like Hitachi or Castrol was enough to reverse a disappointing new season.

With only three points, Lotus finished ninth in the constructors' championship. Beyond the results, the sensations were terrible, with a car that often did not even achieve the necessary times to participate in the races.

With the contribution of the sponsors that had been achieved throughout the previous campaign, the Lotus 107 was developed for 1992 with the aim of ending a trend that threatened the end of the historic team.

Although the design was carried out by Chris Murphy (after the legal problems of Akira Akagi and the Leyton House team that had been in charge of the previous cars), it was even said that it maintained too many similarities with the unsuccessful Lotus 102, beyond of a more stylized appearance and the return to Ford engines with the HB 3.5 V8.

---

[82]pinterest.es

83

The driver squad at least remained stable, with Häkkinen and Herbert the only two drivers throughout the season.

The changes this season at least helped Lotus regain competitiveness, with only Häkkinen failing to qualify in San Marino, with both cars participating on all occasions for the remainder of the season.

Except for the disappointment in San Marino, Häkkinen managed to finish all the races (those in which he did not retire due to mechanical problems) above tenth position, and often in the points zone. This allowed him to add 11 points to finish eighth in the final standings.

As for Herbert, the Briton suffered further reliability problems, retiring in eleven of the sixteen races. In those that he was able to finish, he also finished well positioned, scoring points in South Africa and France, although mechanical problems prevented him from achieving a finishing position better than fifteenth.

With 13 points, Lotus rose to fifth position in the Constructors' World

[83]oneimagef1.wordpress.com

Championship, and at least once again felt slightly competitive and within a competition in which it had saved a first litmus test after the decadent previous season.

For the 1993 season, Lotus improved the 107 by focusing its development on the active suspension.

In previous years, Lotus had been a pioneer team incorporating this technology, and now it intended to do so again by taking it to an even higher level.

However, the effort to improve the active suspension led to the abandonment of the development of other important parts.

84

Herbert continued with the team, but Häkkinen's talent did not go unnoticed by McLaren, who decided to sign the Finn. He was replaced by the Italian Alessandro Zanardi, who had sporadically participated with Jordan in 1991 and with Minardi in 1992. This season, Alex finally got a full program in Formula 1.

---

[84]Pilotoshistoricos.blogspot.com

85

In Herbert's hands, the Lotus 107B showed similar performance to the previous year. Despite the numerous withdrawals, when the races were finished, the Briton did so in points positions, this time adding 11 units that raised him to the ninth position of drivers.

As for Zanardi, he managed to score points by finishing sixth in the second race in Brazil, but he was no longer able to match or improve on that position. In Spa, he suffered a hard accident that caused him a concussion that kept him out of competition for several months.

86

[85]museonicolis.com
[86]the-fastlane.co.uk

He was replaced for the four races by Pedro Lamy, who had been runner-up in Formula 3000. The Portuguese managed to finish in Italy in position 11 and in Japan in position 13.

Lotus finished in sixth position in the constructors' championship with similar sensations to the previous year, stabilizing itself in the championship and moving away from its negative trend. But a historic team like Lotus needed something more.

For the 1994 season, a new Lotus 109 was developed, this time relying on the Mugen-Honda MF-351 HD 3.5 V10 engine. The new car was a refined version of its predecessor, improving the elements that the diminished economy of the team allowed. The wheelbase was shortened and weight was redistributed to lower the center of gravity to make it more manageable, in addition to improving the shape of the sidepods.

87

87pinterest.es

Pedro Lamy continued to replace Zanardi after his accident at the beginning of the season until the return of the Italian, and Johnny Herbert repeated another year with Lotus, continuing with the same driver squad that ended the previous season.

Lamy managed to finish three races around tenth place in his four starts this season, retiring in one of them. After that, Zanardi returned to the championship with slightly lower results than the Portuguese, generally finishing in the last third of the standings. Neither of them got any point for the team.

As for Herbert, he managed to finish in seventh or eighth position as the most frequent result, but in the last few races he decided to try his luck with other teams like Ligier and Benetton.

To replace the Briton, Lotus tested Belgian Philippe Adams in Belgium and Portugal (he dropped out of the Belgian test and finished 16th in the Portuguese). The French Éric Bernard participated in the European Grand Prix finishing 18th and the Finn Mika Salo participated in the last two tests in Japan and Australia (tenth in the Japanese test and retiring in the Australian race).

This instability on the driver's grid was a clear example of the general disorder of the team, which ended the season without scoring any points, sunk in the manufacturers' standings.

These sporting results, together with the team's financial problems, meant the end of a historic team, which had won seven constructors' and six drivers' championships, and which finally decided to retire from competition, abandoning a discipline that it had managed to dominate in the past.

The return of Lotus to Formula 1 in 2010

Sixteen years after the official withdrawal of Lotus from Formula 1, the brand returned to the highest motorsport competition causing a great furor among fans. One of the most historic brands returned to the circuits.

Lotus returned in 2010 under the direction of 1Malaysia F1 Team Sdn Bhd, a company that had obtained permission from Lotus to participate under its name, occupying the place that BMW Sauber vacated in the competition (Sauber did not sell its place, but who temporarily withdrew and left his space to Lotus).

The base of operations was ten miles from the official Lotus factory base in England, so the team participated under dual Anglo-Malay nationality.

The team returned under the name of Lotus Racing, since it did not have the necessary rights to participate with the classic Team Lotus (something that it would achieve the following year). The Malaysian government got involved in the project to promote Proton, the Malaysian car company that owns Lotus Cars.

The Lotus T127 was the single-seater with which the brand returned to a Formula 1 that had changed a lot since its last participation. Its development started exceedingly late, with the factory still under construction at the end of 2009.

Design led by Mike Gascoyne, the Lotus T127 used 2010 Cosworth CA V8 engines for a car that was built against the clock and under pressure from the name they represented.

88

The main driver for this new stage was Jarno Trulli. The Italian already had a long career in Formula 1 since he debuted in 1997 with Minardi.

After half a season with Minardi, he went on to drive for Prost where he got his first points, a team in which he spent two more full years until 1999. After that he continued two more years with Jordan, where he continued to progress, improving his final ranking in the World Cup. pilots up to ninth place and approaching the podium on numerous occasions.

In 2002 and 2003 he was part of the Mild Seven Renault team where he achieved his first podium in Germany in his second year with the French team, after which he spent a long five-year season with Toyota where he added five more podiums to his record and achieved his best final position in a championship: 7th.

The second driver was Heikki Kovalainen. The promising Finnish runner-up in the GP2 Series in 2005 began his Formula 1 career in 2007 with Renault, scoring a podium finish in Japan and finishing seventh in the final standings.

---

[89]skysport.com

After that, he drove for McLaren for two seasons, adding two more podium finishes and taking his first victory in his first year with the English team. After finishing seventh again, 2009 was a more difficult year at McLaren, without returning to the podium, after which he became part of the new Lotus project.

The results of the season were typical of a team that had been hastily created, often finishing at the bottom of the standings at every race, both Trulli and Kovalainen. The best position all year was 12th for the Finn in Japan, and neither driver was able to score points.

In this way, Lotus finished in tenth position in the constructors' championship, with the merit of having surpassed the other rookie teams (HRT and Virgin), but far from the expectations of the name they represented.

At least that year the team was able to celebrate the 500th Grand Prix at the European Grand Prix.

In 2011, the Malaysian team obtained the license to use the classic name of Team Lotus, so fans of the brand consider that this was the true year of the comeback and not the previous one.

This time the team chose to use Renault RS27-2011 engines and used a transmission used by Red Bull Technologies for a Lotus T128 that, beyond the adjustments required by regulations (roll bar and more solid air intakes), was still one step ahead. behind the main cars in the category.

The clearest example was that the Lotus T128 did not incorporate the KERS energy regeneration system, so it was left without that extra energy that the system generated by taking advantage of the kinetic energy of the braking process.

91

Trulli and Kovalainen repeated as drivers for a season that presented itself with low expectations.

The results were similar to the previous season, and even slightly

91carpixel.net

worse, finishing in the last positions of the classification in many of the races. The best position at the end of a race was this time position 13, achieved by Trulli in Australia and Monaco and by Kovalainen in Italy.

Again without any point, Lotus finished in tenth position only ahead of HRT and Virgin, with the insufficient satisfaction of being the best team of the worst classified.

The poor results intensified the dispute between the team and the Lotus Cars company, with the company assuring that the Formula 1 team did not make proper and agreed use of the brand. Although the Formula 1 team won the High Court trial, it decided to dispense with its agreement with Lotus and the Malaysian team opted to run as Caterham from the following year.

However, this was not the end of Lotus in Formula 1. The brand, which had sponsored Renault this year (finishing the French team in fifth position), was about to move up a notch in its partnership with the French team. .

Last leg of Lotus in its partnership with Renault

After the disassociation of Lotus Cars with the Malaysian team now transformed into the Caterham F1 Team, Lotus continued its official career in Formula 1 through the Renault team with which it had already collaborated in 2011. The French team, in decline after having enjoyed his glorious years with Fernando Alonso, officially abandoned the competition although it served as a platform and infrastructure to continue in it through the Lotus F1 Team.

The Lotus E20 was designed at Renault's Enstone base in a project led by James Allison, Martin Tolliday, Dirk de Beer and Naoki Tokunaga. It obviously continued to use Renault engines and its design was based on swinging ride height, with a device that varied the ride height during acceleration and braking.

In this way, weight distribution and aerodynamics were improved, providing better maneuverability and handling. However, this device was banned by the FIA, as movable aerodynamic devices were not allowed, and Lotus had to face this season without the new technology it had been entrusted with.

For this new stage of Lotus, the team hired Kimi Räikkönen, bringing about the return of the Finnish champion after two years focused on the World Rally Championship (finishing tenth in both).

Kimi's long career had begun in 2001 with Sauber, being quickly signed by McLaren, a team with which he shared five years, achieving world runner-up twice.

In 2007 he signed for Ferrari, a team with which he managed to become world champion and with which he spent two more not so prosperous years, being third in 2008 and sixth in 2009.

After passing through the rally, the Finnish driver returned to

Formula 1 through the new Lotus under the shadow of Renault.

[93]

The second driver this season was Frenchman Romain Grosjean, who had already been a test driver the previous season for Renault under the name Lotus Renault GP where he had also been champion of the GP2 Series and the GP2 Asia Series.

94

---

[93]20minutos.es
[94]motormundial.es

Despite the ban on the innovative ride height adjustment system, Lotus was competitive from the start of the competition, with Räikkönen scoring points in the first two rounds in Australia and Malaysia and finishing on the podium in rounds four and five in Bahrain and Spain. After that, the Finn managed to continue scoring points in practically all the races, and added three more consecutive podiums in Germany, Hungary and Belgium. As the culmination of a good season, Räikkönen achieved victory in Abu Dhabi.

With 207 points, the Finn signed a good year finishing third in the world championship, only behind the unattainable Vettel and Alonso.

Grosjean's debut in Formula 1 was more discreet, but despite his inexperience he managed three podiums and recurring points to add 96 points and finish in eighth position. Collectively, Lotus moved up to fourth behind Red Bull and Ferrari, bettering Renault's last-year position (for part of the championship, it was even fighting for runner-up). This was a hopeful start to this new stage of Lotus. Despite this good sporting start with the Renault infrastructure, the financial results were not of the same caliber, with the loss of numerous sponsors that complicated the continuity of the team.

With sporting optimism but limited financial resources, Lotus developed the Lotus E21 for the 2012 season, characterized by the "duck nose" that broke the aesthetics of most cars on the grid. The FIA allowed the use of a small piece of carbon fiber to improve the aesthetics of these fronts so little appreciated by fans, but Lotus chose not to use it, since it did not improve aerodynamics and meant a small increase in weight. The development of the car this year focused on the DRS system, the mobile spoiler that took advantage of the airflow generated by the car in front, granting greater speed to favor overtaking.

95

Räikkönen and Grosjean repeated as official drivers with the hope of repeating the performance of the previous season and, why not, improve it and aspire to fight for the championship.

The season couldn't have started better, with Räikkönen taking victory in Australia despite starting seventh on the starting grid, beating Vettel's almighty Red Bull and the talented Alonso's Ferrari.

Following a seventh-place finish in Malaysia, the Finn racked up three consecutive second-place podium finishes in what was a superb start to the season.

Meanwhile, Grosjean continued to score points in all races, and in the fourth test in Bahrain he took third place, which put both Lotuses on the podium.

Although Lotus was unable to repeat victory, the trend of podium finishes continued throughout the year, with Räikkönen taking a total of seven podiums and Grosjean six.

With Red Bull dominating the competition, winning almost every race and out of reach, with these results Lotus at least aspired to runner-up and competed against leading teams like Mercedes and Ferrari.

However, despite the good results, organizational and financial problems continued to harass the team, which accumulated millions in losses.

In the middle of the season, technical director James Allison left the team (later he would be signed by Ferrari), being replaced by Nick Chester. Genii Capital, a group that owned 98% of the shares, began

---

[96]uncafeconserena.com

negotiations for the sale of shares that did not materialize.

With this internal instability, Kimi Räikkönen missed the last two races (there were also accusations that he was not getting paid), and was replaced by Hekki Kovalainen who finished 14th in the last two events.

With 315 points, Lotus finished fourth in the constructors' championship, very close to Ferrari and Mercedes, in a year that, like the previous one, showed good sporting performance, but continued financial difficulties.

For the 2014 season, internal instability continued with the resignation of Éric Boullier as team manager, being replaced by Gerard Lopez.

Nick Chester's Lotus E22 for this season used Renault's new turbocharged 1.6-litre V6 engine to suit the new hybrid era in Formula 1 that combined electric power alongside traditional combustion as a power source.

Renault showed problems adapting to these new power units that manifested themselves in poor reliability.

The development of the car, which was characterized by having a forked nose, was complicated, forcing the team to miss the first pre-season tests in Jerez, and to start the season in a hurry.

97

With Kimi Räikkönen returning to Ferrari, Grosjean's partner in this edition was Pastor Maldonado. The Venezuelan had made his debut and driven for Williams since 2011 after winning the GP2 Series, taking a victory with the legendary British team, although finishing 15th as the best result in the drivers' classification in an era in which Williams was far from his best times in the competition.

98

[97]f1aldia.com
[98]soymotor.com

Internal problems, the departure of a champion like Räikkönen and the revolution of the hybrid era was a cocktail that Lotus suffered with a decrease in performance.

The team stopped aspiring to win races and even fight for podiums, settling for points, which became a difficult task.

Grosjean managed to add eight points with two eighth positions in Spain and Monaco, while Maldonado managed to add two points in the United States finishing ninth.

The ban on the FRIC system that Mercedes and Lotus had started developing since 2011 also dealt a severe setback for the team.

This technology joined the front and rear suspensions to compensate each other, giving a better balance.

With all this, Lotus fell to the bottom of the manufacturer's standings, surpassing only Marussia, Sauber and Caterham. The team, which had fought for victories in previous years and dreamed of being able to aspire to a championship, now obtained radically different results.

In 2015, Lotus decided to use the Mercedes PU106 Hybrid engine, seeing that the German brand seemed to have adapted well to the new hybrid era.

The Lotus E23 Hybrid was the first Enstone-built car not to use Renault engines since 1994 since Benetton opted to be powered by Ford.

Grosjean and Maldonado continued to be the official drivers for the team, hoping that the new power units from Mercedes would reverse the performance of the previous season.

Despite the disastrous debut in Australia with both cars being involved in an accident and having to retire, Lotus improved in performance throughout the year. However, the new engines were not enough to recover the trend of previous years. The team at least did manage to score more frequently. Both drivers managed to finish between sixth and eighth in relative comfort, at least when the frequent reliability problems did not present themselves.

Grosjean even managed to take the podium in Belgium, second only to the unstoppable Mercedes of Hamilton and Rosberg, giving Lotus cause for joy and optimism.

The Frenchman finished 11th in the final drivers' standings with 51 points, while Maldonado finished 14th with 27 points.

Overall, Lotus rose to sixth position and took a step forward from the disastrous previous season.

99gasolinesuper.es

However, despite this slight recovery, Lotus no longer continued with its project. Renault officially returned to the championship and that meant the final departure of Lotus in Formula 1.

In this way, a brand that had forged its legend by winning seven constructors' and six drivers' championships was definitively leaving the competition.

Gone were the times of Jim Clark, Graham Hill, Jochen Rindt, Emerson Fittipaldi or Mario Andretti, and the innovations of Colin Chapman that changed Formula 1 forever.

The competition will always remember this constructor as one of the most decisive and significant in its history. Will Lotus be able to return in the future to continue continuing the pages of its history in this wonderful competition?

THANKS

To all of you who encourage my love of motorsports, which has been the germ of this work.

To all of you who enjoy Formula 1 and make this a shared passion.

To all those who have made me any notes or corrections (and who will continue to do so) to create a more truthful and accurate title.

To all the graphic resources referred to throughout the book, for making this text attractive.

To all of you who send me your opinions and make this book something collective.

Many thanks.
Charles Sanz.

MORE BOOKS BY CHARLES SANZ

THE HISTORY OF FORMULA 1 TO THE RHYTHM OF FAST LAP

Formula 1 is the obsession to be **the fastest on the asphalt**. It is the passion for that split second that separates success from failure.

We enjoy its cutting-edge **technology**, seeking to polish that piece that allows you to start a few thousandths from the stopwatch; develop the most powerful engine to make the car fly on the track or control the wind to turn it into a few extra kilometers per hour through aerodynamics.

And of course, we enjoy the **battles on the track** at the limit between life and death, overtaking off the track at more than 300 km / h, pianos devoured to the extreme assuming the risk of an accident or off the track.

But above all, Formula 1 is its history. Let's face it, there's no race we see without bringing back memories of the glorious past. You don't enjoy this sport so much without knowing its route, its history, the greatness that one day was and will continue to be and that comes back to our minds every time the engines roar. It would not be covered with that halo of heroism without those times in which those heroes through the control of time and speed became legends on the asphalt.

MORE BOOKS BY CHARLES SANZ

THE HISTORY OF FERRARI IN THE FORMULA 1 TO THE RHYTHM OF FAST LAP

When Enzo Ferrari set out to create his own motorsport team, he did not give up until he succeeded and took it to absolute success. In the early years, it would not take long to achieve glory through Alberto Ascari and fighting with and against Fangio. In the early years of the championship, Ferrari always managed to be at the top of Formula 1 through drivers such as Mike Hawthorn, Phil Hill and John Surtees, becoming a team that was always a candidate for victory. Between 1964 and 1974, the rise of British brands complicated Ferrari's trajectory in a complicated period, but Niki Lauda would end up becoming the savior who would lead the Scuderia back to winning championships.

After a new dark period where the championships resisted despite having drivers with the talent of Nigel Mansell or Alain Prost, a hero came to the rescue of the Italian team to provide it with the best years of its history: Michael Schumacher. After the departure of the legendary German, only Kimi Räikkönen managed to extend the triumph of Scuderia Ferrari, despite having champions like Alonso or Vettel.

In these pages you will enjoy the history of the most legendary team in Formula 1 in the form of a simple walk through time and through the keys to its trajectory so that you can enjoy its magnificent past in a light-hearted way.

MORE BOOKS BY CHARLES SANZ

THE HISTORY OF RED BULL IN FORMULA 1 AT RHYTHM OF FAST LAP

Who could have guessed that an energy drink brand could come to reign supreme in Formula 1? Red Bull's beginnings were as a sponsor through Sauber. Thus, with its financial contribution to the Swiss team, Red Bull achieved the team's first podium through German Heinz-Harald Frentzen, in addition to adding the brand's name to the team that saw the debut of a future champion: Kimi Räikkönen.

However, Red Bull's racing ambitions went further than that. In 2005, it bought the Jaguar team to create its own team. Who would have thought that this risky maneuver could end in success? Then came the moments of glory: David Coulthard's first podium finish in Monaco, or Toro Rosso's first victory at Monza and Red Bull's first victory in China by a Sebastian Vettel who ended up being key to Red Bull's golden era.

But Red Bull is much more than Sebastian Vettel's glory days. This book shows the trajectory of Red Bull in Formula 1 in a simple, light and through its main keys so you can enjoy wonderful memories or learn the past of this great team.

MORE BOOKS BY CHARLES SANZ

THE HISTORY OF RENAULT IN FORMULA 1 AT RHYTHM OF FAST LAP

In these pages you will discover or remember the origins of Renault, a whole story of overcoming from the ridiculed "yellow kettle" with its frequent explosions of white smoke to the first victory of Jean-Pierre Jabouille and the consecration of the turbo in Formula 1.

You will enjoy the arrival at Renault of Alain Prost, one of the best drivers in history, and his impact on the development of the team. You will also walk through Renault's golden era as an engine supplier, in its perfect partnership with the Williams of legendary drivers such as Nigel Mansell, Damon Hill or Ayrton Senna, or the Benetton of Michael Schumacher.

You will enjoy the glory days of the constructor after the arrival of Fernando Alonso to the team and the best years of its history, as well as the subsequent decline and the nightmare of crashgate, the provoked accident of Nelson Piquet Jr. that shook the foundations of the team. Finally, you will return to the years of uncertainty in its alliance with Lotus, subsequent sale of the team and its new return with the aim of, progressively, trying to recover performance in a convulsive hybrid era with the goal of returning to its best times.

MORE BOOKS BY CHARLES SANZ

THE HISTORY OF MCLAREN IN FORMULA 1 AT RHYTHM OF FAST LAP

In these pages you will discover or remember the origins of Mclaren, the team that Bruce himself created to continue his career in Formula 1. In 1966, the Bruce McLaren Motor Racing team debuted in the competition, achieving its first victory two years later. However, in 1970 a fatal accident took the magnificent Bruce from us. Instead of disappearing after the loss of its founder, the McLaren team continued in the competition achieving its first great triumph thanks to the talent of the Brazilian Emerson Fittipaldi. Aboard a McLaren, James Hunt starred in one of the most spectacular seasons of Formula 1 in his confrontation with Niki Lauda's Ferrari in 1976. But it was Alain Prost and Ayrton Senna, teammates and eternal rivals on the track, who led McLaren to become the most powerful team in Formula 1. McLaren was no longer able to dominate as it did between 1988 and 1991, but its goal was always to be at the top of the competition, and drivers like Mika Häkkinen and Lewis Hamilton proved that a McLaren was always to be feared on the racetrack. Although its recent past is somewhat dark, the history of this great team has shown that McLaren will always have a reserved place among the best teams in Formula 1.

MORE BOOKS BY CHARLES SANZ

THE HISTORY OF WILLIAMS IN FORMULA 1 AT RHYTHM OF FAST LAP

The Williams team is undoubtedly one of the most legendary in Formula 1 due to its long and successful history, with humble beginnings followed by an exciting rise to glory, with its subsequent fall and collapse.

This generated wonderful stories to remember, with Alan Jones pushing the team to the top and Clay Regazzoni achieving the first victory, or Carlos Reutemann fighting with a whole Nelson Piquet who would later also end up being part of Williams. The magic of Williams would lead Rosberg to be an atypical champion, and to attract the attention of legends such as Alain Prost or Nigel Mansell, who would end up being seduced by one of the most sophisticated and technological single-seaters in the history of Formula 1, capable of beating the almighty McLaren.

Even one of the greatest legends of Formula 1, the Brazilian Ayrton Senna, showed his recurring desire to drive for Williams, and his name would be linked to the British team for eternity. Only a motor racing prodigy like Michael Schumacher seemed to be able to stop the hegemony of Williams, having to resort to the limits of sportsmanship to compete with drivers like Damon Hill or Jacques Villeneuve.

MORE BOOKS BY CHARLES SANZ

THE PRIDE OF BEING FERRARI DRIVER – VOLUME 1

DO YOU KNOW THE HISTORY OF THE RIDERS WHO STARTED BUILDING THE FERRARI LEGEND IN FORMULA 1?

Scuderia Ferrari is undoubtedly one of the most legendary in the history of Formula 1. It is the team with the most championships won and the only one that has participated in all editions.

This means that all the drivers who managed to sit in a Scuderia Ferrari car ended up covered by a halo of heroism capable of transcending time. In this volume, we will take a walk through the stories of all the drivers who participated in the team during the 1950s: Ascari, the first great Ferrari legend; José Froilán González and the first victory for the Scuderia; Giuseppe Farina, the first F1 champion; Hawthorn and Collins' friendship to the detriment of Musso; Peter Collins and his enormous chivalry; Fangio and his talent beyond the mark...

MORE BOOKS BY CHARLES SANZ

THE HISTORY OF WORLD MOTORCYCLE CHAMPIONSHIP TO THE RHYTHM OF FAST LAP

MotoGP is the obsession to be the fastest on the asphalt on two wheels. It is the passion of riding an elite motorcycle and being part of the machine, sticking to it on every straight and tumbling on every curve. But above all, the world motorcycle championship is its history. There is no career that does not take us back to its glorious past, its legendary battles and exciting races etched in memory. You don't enjoy this sport so much without knowing its route and its evolution.

The legend of Giacomo Agostini, the absolute dominance of MV Augusta, the American hegemony with Freddie Spencer, Eddie Lawson and Wayne Rainey, the legacy of Doohan, the era of Valentino Rossi, the reign of the Spanish pilots ...

That is the objective of this book: a simple walk through its history to remember or learn about its origins and the years that mythologized this sport, to feel the weight of its past, thus adding another dose of passion to the best motorcycling championship in the world.

Made in the USA
Middletown, DE
25 January 2023

22901542R00077